Kathmandu

Kathmandu

Anuja Ghimire

Kathmandu
Copyright © 2020 Anuja Ghimire

All Rights Reserved
Published by Unsolicited Press
Printed in the United States of America.
First Edition.

No part of this book may be used or reproduced in any manner whatsoever without written permission except in the case of brief quotations embodied in critical articles or reviews.

Attention schools and businesses: for discounted copies on large orders, please contact the publisher directly.

For information contact:
Unsolicited Press
Portland, Oregon
www.unsolicitedpress.com
orders@unsolicitedpress.com
619-354-8005

Cover Design: Kathryn Gerhardt
Editor: Bekah Stogner

ISBN: 978-1-950730-51-3

Contents

When Rajiv was blown up	7
Revolution, 2046 B.S.[1]	9
Nakabandi (Blockade)[2]	10
The royals, 2058 B.S.[3]	12
The first flight	13
Saffron	14
My little brother says he has to escape	15
Orlando	16
My heart skips ten beats a second	17
God, five-years-old, saves my life, 2072 B.S.[4]	18
The Mosquito Net, Earthquake, 2072 B.S.[5]	19
Dancing when neighbors are drowning	20
Purple rain, 2050 B.S.[6]	21
Summer of endless rain	22
Semolina pudding	23
My baby starts kindergarten on total solar eclipse	25
For winter, for spring	26
I dream of a river, 2049 B.S.[8]	28
Lineage	29
A young woman says "I want to speak English like you"	30
Twenty-five years later, I think happiness is understanding	31

When Rajiv was blown up

after Rajiv Gandhi's assassination in 1991

Before her belly would caress
and press the bomb in her sari,
she gave the man a garland
for his neck and bent
to touch his feet

It was just the way my father touched
the power button on our television's waist
as it shook on the wooden dresser

My mother had taught me
enough words to understand
the man was shocked
and killed in the same instant

I'd loved enough to know
each night I wanted to sleep
with a quiet stomach,
watching the faces I've always known

I'd lived long enough to learn
of the inventions shared,
like the television and bombs,
blasting terror in tiny brains

As my mother bent to tuck me in bed
the night the woman blew up Rajiv,
I searched the pleats of her sari
for the shrapnel of fairy tales

Revolution, 2046 B.S.[1]

In the nights of ordered lights out,
when even the flicker of a candle
was a giveaway
I wrapped the torso of my doll
in an orange scarf
the sari was without pleats
and the loose end
wouldn't cover her head
but I wanted to show her off anyway
to my father with a pillow over his ears
my mother hunting for shards
in grains of rice
her nose buried in the bamboo plate

my brother with his hands rusting like his toy cars
sister who hummed jingles because
she could still replay the television in her mind
but not the officers stomping down the street
inches away from my window
they said bullets feel hot on little necks

---

[1] Nepali year in Nepali calendar 1989

Nakabandi (Blockade)[2]

I am waiting
for sugar and oil
when it is finally my turn,
the polythene bags fly in the air
I've skipped homework to claim my spot
now lost to the plastic flutter
that aimed for the moon
I know your dance
my calves are only stronger
because of the stomps of *Bharat Natyam*
ta thai tatha thai tak
I know your song
my tongue is only softer
after the *riyaz* of our scale
sa re ga ma pa dha ni sa
I know your arms
they spread wider than mine
to grasp Everest by her forehead
she won't topple
so your feet push the soil
with a bit of the crusty earth
towards me with each hushed step
I know you will break our pact
and free will is an act--
it's flavored medicine to swallow pride

---

[2] India's blockades in 2049 B.S. /1989 and 2072 B.S./2015

I know that if I vomit,
the splatter on your shoes
will only land on my cheeks
so I wait for sugar and oil

The royals, 2058 B.S.[3]

Words were warped in the wires
when you called anyway
I said the assassination changes everything
milk was poisoned, water was ink
sitar strings on the radio were hollow dirges
I remember
vibrato of your voice
vanishing of laughter
you spoke of the funeral procession
beds of marigolds floating to the temple
how they used a doll's face for the queen's head
so we'd remember her beauty
but men who'd lined up had cut their hair,
marked the path in tears
the nightly news on television were sandalwood pyre
one by one, the royals lit up by the river
we never talked about the bullet holes sealed beneath the flowers

---

[3] 2001

The first flight

we looked out the windows and not at each other
the taxi skidded and bounced, with it, my heart

my mother's sank with each turbulence
father sighed and exhaled his sorrow

in the trunk, my two Samsonite suitcases swayed
instant noodles, notebooks, staplers, and pens too cramped to move

when the driver hit the brakes and my mother's forehead collided with the seat,
she whimpered and released the tears

before I settled my forehead under her chin,
I watched her lips quiver and mouth
don't go, don't go, don't go

Saffron

I flutter when I dance
and shiver when I drive
my fingers create lotus, deer and Shiva
How far is Houston from Victoria City?
prayers of my palm, poetry in my eyes
the sky is so big, the roads are so wide
I don't melt here
my saffron, your orange
when I push carts and displace
cans from the shelves,
I ache, I stomp
my fingers create the rain
and reach for the milk
when I am not watched,
I make art in Wal-Mart

My little brother says he has to escape

I tell my brother I have a poem for him
really just a string of words in a language
we never spoke at home
It shows me choking on my laptop
kohl drops landing on the keyboard
Babu steals time at work to ask me what it is
I have turned off the lights
He has opened up the window
when his rubber slippers snap
He is a little boy on my back, carried home from school
when I am six and he is five
we wear the same clothes and Ma can't tell us apart
until I ask, "Which one of us is *babu?*"
He comes home late with clever excuses
pulling stories out of his pockets,
hiding cricket balls and smudging grass stains
I fight with him on the day someone tells me
that the Third World War will start any time
fearmongers claw at my imagination
I stay by the window that Sunday my brother is late from school
He comes home with a broken arm
It's swollen like a radish, he never cries
We don't fight again
He plays boy games, and I quietly plan an escape
He grows a beard without my notice
I tell him I have a poem for him
and ask not to be forgotten

Orlando

I need not complete this poem
in the Milky Way, it would take 100 centuries for one star to get to another
let's break the words apart—lend me a hammer
even the nuclei don't matter
today, my children hugged the lady who bagged four gallons of organic milk
        and blew her kisses
"Beautiful innocence," Kim said, her nametag sending light back to the ceiling
so what if the girls know what love is
only humans feel embarrassed, veins betray the emotion on our cheeks
What color is despair?
"A bad guy," my six-year-old said about the scattered shattered glass around
        the tree carefully separated from the concrete of the parking lot
In a game of telephone, words alter truth with each whisper in a new ear
Mr. Rogers said, "Always look for the helper"
but the flowers in my heart didn't last a spring
I want to keep my little girls in my arms, but they blossom at the window

My heart skips ten beats a second

When November is warm and sunny,
my coal-black ringlets dance with the lone star air
I think of my mother and her long-lost curls
her strands are chopped and frigid-
burgundy and gray like Kathmandu frost
she wears my father's woolen cap,
wraps herself in a cotton sari-always red
clings to a flannel shawl that smells of *ghee*
the fog seeps into her veins
the cement lies still beneath her hurrying feet
the only distance she can run is
to the warmth of the kerosene stove
my arrhythmic mother prays for me
when she reads the notice left by the people's warriors,
she wonders if my head still hurts from reading too much
sometimes, words steal all the fire away
amidst the jute sacks of rice and polythene bags of sugar, as per the order,
she waits for the ten guests, and prays in protest
against three days and three nights of house arrest
tonight, the tenants have fled, and the dog is set free.
her only freedom lies seven seas away, in my dancing curls

God, five-years-old, saves my life, 2072 B.S.[4]

my daughter announced she was God
as Earth turned into tides

she'd seen fear, mine,
when I didn't have enough hands
to wrap around one child,
and also hold another

when I dug the ground with my heels
to plant the three of us like Everest,
my faith was shaking, and she knew

then, she let the land swing like a temple bell
dust rose to our foreheads like a prayer

my God still stopped the quakes with her breath
until I, too, had two right hands and two left

---

[4] 2015

The Mosquito Net, Earthquake, 2072 B.S.[5]

on Wednesday,
my mother-in-law read in the Sunday paper
about another grandmother

the woman could not tear off
mosquito net with her bare hands,
her knees on the edge of the day bed
when the earth cracked
the baby's wails broke his mother's fingers
she'd clawed at the net for fifty-nine seconds

the story was ink
only because the grandfather was on the porch
his chin still higher than the ground

that night,
we lined up our four pairs of sandals
on the canvas tent's border
the hardened skin of our feet, almost seismic, measured tremors
we watched our children's closed eyes,
swatted at the mosquitoes with our palms
like a rain of prayers[5]

---

[5] 2015

Dancing when neighbors are drowning

When the mourners gathered like hills and wept
their foreheads touched their knees

for two hundred Saturdays
in the same living room
they had leaned on cushions,
swallowed chicken chili with weak rum
and played flush with him

weekly, his cheekbones rose like skeletons of fish
his breathing descended from a mountain
then his eyes fell inside him with a woodpecker's abandon

once, before I had only known him on his way to death,
he had tousled my hair and given it a hurricane

I remember the monsoon of the thirteenth day
my beetle feet under the umbrella

although they howled next door and my mother
had warned me against singing,
I had twirled and forgotten grief in the balcony

Purple rain, 2050 B.S.[6]

on the afternoon of sudden rain
I could just reach the small fold
of my mother's belly
I'd watch the brown pocket of her skin
as circles of shadows danced
and freed the scent of sidewalk cement
my first umbrella held me
the free end of my mother's cotton sari
which only drenched me more
but colored every drop sliding through
my forehead

---

[6] 1993

Summer of endless rain

for Pie Lee Tang and Victoria Tang

After my neighbor died in spring,
her daughter gave me a key
to water plants in the backyard

There our fences meet

Victoria had thought she would stay longer
this time with her old mother
and the blossoms

Every sunset, I reach in the envelope for the key

Mrs. Tang leaves her front yard
in her walker. The wheels bump on the grass.
The metal bars thud in her pale, spotted hands.

Mrs. Tang watches my daughters grow in the driveway

I pull one baby from the stroller
and set her on a tricycle
Another crawls on our porch
and hops on a scooter

Victoria rakes fallen oak leaves like every November
and clears the way

When her mother reaches the mailbox, it rains.

Semolina pudding

When the moon is less full by one night
I look up but I don't wonder
if my brother is watching it, too

his sky has the sun now
always equally circular
nights like these, he's sipping morning tea
I'm holding him in poetry

I want to tell him
how I heated up ghee and sautéed semolina
earlier in the afternoon
when he was dreaming
I added milk and sugar
just the way I did twenty-five years ago
the first meal I ever cooked

Do you remember, brother?
the recipe in the back of a textbook
when the tape rolls, our kitchen is dark
only the kerosene stove and ghee burn
two kinds of yellow
haluwa[7] creams

---

[7] semolina pudding

I could do anything for you, brother
So I didn't burn the house for a meal
Now, love is all kinds of abstract
I go back

To when our afternoons didn't have a twelve-hour layer
I lower the sun and place it outside the window
and push the stove's lever
The flames cup the frying pan's edges
as I break the lumps
now golden brown
I do not turn off the fire just yet
My brother is the brightest moon.

My baby starts kindergarten on total solar eclipse

five years, I tried to catch a star with a butterfly net
at seven fifty a.m., she waves goodbye
I take the air she has moved in the room
raise my hand
unlearn cradle-hold
when I leave, her half smile shows four missing teeth
I breathe in
the hallway, glass door, parking lot
in my backyard, shadows of a half-eaten sun are many moons
they have warned me not to stare directly at the burning sky
I'd forgotten my eyes
on a mermaid water bottle, heart-shaped lunchbox, a flower-laced backpack
and each pothole on the highway

For winter, for spring

1.
Of *Karomia gigas*,
there are only six trees
Tanzanians keep a watch on their seeds
and guard the breeze

2.
My backyard has two peach and plum plants
trunks thinner than my wrists
only last spring, they began to bloom
with my daughters' watercolor brush strokes
but my body is here on a lease

3.
The man who hummed held his baby
like an apple tree carries hearts on its branch tips
past the engines that paused fire in the school parking lot
he moved with an afternoon lullaby on his lips

4.
On the radio, a man says thirty words
about a three-year-old
girl who never stood by that tree
a hundred feet behind the house that dawn
—of that man who lugged her across the ocean
and filled her lungs with milk

5.
I don't know the names of 60,000 trees
Sidhhartha shed suffering under *Bodhi's* shadow
I am seven seas away from *Peepal's* leaves
where should I close my eyes and rest my knees?

6.
The man returns with another child in his shade
but the same song for the sleeping blossom;
they leave winter's parade

7.
My hand out the waiting window
reaches for my daughters' faces
brings back spring and silk

I dream of a river, 2049 B.S.[8]

The fishbone in my throat

You and I on a mound
Soil frozen on a rock near the forest

You near the pine cones

I rooted

Remember how they waited by the waters

Eyes on every leaf

But for a breath-long moment

They all rested on my neck

Funneling all the light of the sun

The bone was thin, diagonal

Nobody knows about blood falling inside
I think you knew about mine

My interrupted swallows

How we all watched the gold thickening

Again, everyone glanced at me ripple by ripple

When I wanted to eat the moon, you unhinged my jaw

My lips returned the bone to the fish in the red river

---

[8] 1992

Lineage

Before I met them, my grandmothers were stars
my grandfather ran on the hills when snow fell
for the sun, he moved his love to the plains
there, my father held his new bride's head, bent under *Peepal's* shade every
    dusk
he packed their marriage in a tin trunk to the valley
where my feet grew on the bowl of the mountains
every year, I folded words by the sleeves, neck, and body until I fit
in two suitcases
when I could see beyond my mother's forehead, she released
me across the oceans

to the land where buildings fell but dreams still climbed on steel
tonight, my daughter stains a pillow on her bed and says when people laugh at
    her, she is alone on earth, everyone in the galaxy forever looks down

A young woman says "I want to speak English like you"

she wants to hold my foreign words on the precipice of her tongue
    like Seinfeld's *Babu* and Simpson's *Apu*
       to unfurl them as a party trick
"*Howe aar yuuu?*"
but the cloak of her intonations slides again, again
she stands can't-see-the-change-in-your-cheeks meters away
flicks her chin-length hair
       after the west wind knocks me down on my cubicle, I am three, and
           my forehead hits the wooden desk,
       number 2 *Nataraj* pencil dots my white, ironed uniform sleeve
       elbow smudges on my first alphabets:
           the circular egg, police stick, monkey's tail, an demon's moustache क
           that I learned to write dreaming
           the broken triangle with a tummy stitch A, A, A that I wake up
               mumbling
lightning of her question shrinks her in a flash, too
    she is salmon hue, bare on her mother's lap
    an "o" escapes from her wet lips when her mother
    says "aa"
    and still claps, claps, claps
    the baby sits up straight, syllable by syllable
    and stretches into the young woman
    laughing alone in the office
    near telephones that ring, ring, ring
    the same in any language

Twenty-five years later, I think happiness is understanding

three winters, I went back to my father's old village
to watch twenty pigeons become sixteen
my chin on the wooden ledge, knees on the floor
eyes half drowned in the aluminum pan
their beaks' rhythmic dip on the silver water
my cheek landed on the railing with each drowsy nod
I knew before he left, my grandfather had ordered the pigeons to not fly
not even as high as the papaya tree near the house
the sun was the thickest in Janakpur just for my asthmatic grandfather
all the cows called him *baa,* too, and remembered their way home
when his hands tremored in the orange sky, their hoove unearthed the path to
        the fence
only when my *Baa* rained fistfuls of grain for the pigeons, three chickens also
        came, and then, the moon
every time I write this poem, *Baa* moves a flock of stars that silently drop on
        the white space of this page, and the pigeons are free

Notes

"When Rajiv was Blown Up" was published in "The Good Men Project" website and nominated for Best of the Net

"Revolution 2046" was published in *Pilgrimage.*

"Nakabandi (blockade)" was published in *Straight Forward Poetry.*

"Saffron" and "Summer of Endless Rain" were published in *Glass-A Journal of Poetry.*

"My little brother says he has to escape" and "My heart skips 10 beats a second" were published in *Red River Review.*

"My baby starts kindergarten on total solar eclipse" and "For Winter, For Spring" were published in *Mothers Always Write*

"The mosquito net" was published in *No Extra Words*

"Orlando" was published in *Literary Orphans*

"Semolina Pudding" was published in *Sunlight Press*

"I dream of a river, 2049" was published in *Eco Theo Review*

"A young woman says 'I want to speak English like you'"* was published in *UCity Review* as a part of noteworthy poet feature

About the Author

Anuja Ghimire was born in Kathmandu, Nepal and came to America to attend college. She began seriously writing and publishing since 2008. A Best of the Net and Pushcart nominee, she has published poetry, creative nonfiction and flash fiction in the U.S., Canada, Nepal, and the U.K. Most recently, her work appeared in *Finished Creatures (UK)*, *Glass: A journal of poetry*, *Medusa's Laughs Press Microanthology*, and *EcoTheo Review*. She works as a senior publisher in an education-based company near Dallas, Texas. She lives with her husband and two young daughters near Dallas.

About the Press

Unsolicited Press is a small press in Portland, Oregon. The team publishes outstanding poetry, fiction, and creative nonfiction. Learn more at unsolicitedpress.com.

www.ingramcontent.com/pod-product-compliance
Lightning Source LLC
Chambersburg PA
CBHW030142100526
44592CB00011B/1011